5/30/00			

Visual Geography Series®

ISRAEL

...in Pictures

Prepared by
Steve Feinstein

Lerner Publications Company
Minneapolis

Independent Picture Service

A group of students attending the Hebrew University of Jerusalem posed in 1954 in front of their dormitory.

This is an all-new edition of the Visual Geography Series. Previous editions have been published by Sterling Publishing Company, New York City, and some of the original textual information has been retained. New photographs, maps, charts, captions, and updated information have been added. The text has been entirely reset in 10/12 Century Textbook.

LIBRARY OF CONGRESS CATALOGING-IN-PUBLICATION DATA

Feinstein, Steve.
  Israel in pictures / prepared by Steve Feinstein.
    p.   cm.—(Visual geography series)
  Rev. ed. of: Israel in pictures / by Peggy Mann and Nina Brodsky.
  Includes index.
  Summary: Text and photographs introduce the ancient and modern history, geography, government, economy, and culture of the biblical country reborn in modern times.
  ISBN 0-8225-1833-3 (lib. bdg.)
  1. Israel. [1. Israel.] I. Mann, Peggy. Israel in pictures. II. Title.   III. Series: Visual geography series (Minneapolis, Minn.)
DS102.95.F45 1988   87-26476
956.94'05—dc19   CIP
                                                  AC

International Standard Book Number: 0-8225-1833-3
Library of Congress Catalog Card Number: 87-26476

VISUAL GEOGRAPHY SERIES®

Publisher
Harry Jonas Lerner
Associate Publisher
Nancy M. Campbell
Senior Editor
Mary M. Rodgers
Editor
Gretchen Bratvold
Illustrations Editors
Karen A. Sirvaitis
Consultants/Contributors
Stephen C. Feinstein
William Siegel
Sandra K. Davis
Designer
Jim Simondet
Cartographer
Carol F. Barrett
Indexer
Sylvia Timian
Production Manager
Richard J. Hannah

Independent Picture Service

Mount Tabor rises beyond new housing for immigrants at Upper Nazareth.

Acknowledgments

Title page photo courtesy of Minneapolis Public Library and Information Center.

Elevation contours adapted from *The Times Atlas of the World*, seventh comprehensive edition (New York: Times Books, 1985).

3   4   5   6   7   8   9   10   97   96   95   94   93   92   91

With the creation of the State of Israel on May 14, 1948, the new nation opened its doors to Jewish immigrants from around the world. These Jews from Yemen were airlifted to Israel during "Operation Magic Carpet."

Contents

LEBANON

Qarn R.

Acre
Carmiel
Capernaum
Sea of Galilee
Haifa
Nazareth
Ein Haud
Atlit
Qishon R.
Afula
Bet She'an

MEDITERRANEAN
SEA

Caesarea
Hadera
Hadera R.

WEST
BANK

Jordan R.

TEL AVIV-JAFFA
Yarqon R.
Ramat Gan
Rehovot
Jerusalem
QUMRAN

GOLAN HEIGHTS

SYRIA

GAZA STRIP
Galilee-Negev Conduit
Hebron
Dead Sea

JORDAN

Beersheba

Besor R.

Yeroham

EGYPT

SINAI PENINSULA

Eilat

Gulf of Aqaba

ISRAEL

N↑

——— District Boundaries

| 0 | 25 | 50 Miles |
| 0 | 25 | 50 Kilometers |

MIDDLE EAST
ISRAEL

20°

20°

40°

20°

40°   60°

INDIAN OCEAN

| 0 | 500 Miles |
| 0 | 500 Kilometers |

METRIC CONVERSION CHART
To Find Approximate Equivalents

WHEN YOU KNOW:	MULTIPLY BY:	TO FIND:
AREA		
acres	0.41	hectares
square miles	2.59	square kilometers
CAPACITY		
gallons	3.79	liters
LENGTH		
feet	30.48	centimeters
yards	0.91	meters
miles	1.61	kilometers
MASS (weight)		
pounds	0.45	kilograms
tons	0.91	metric tons
VOLUME		
cubic yards	0.77	cubic meters
TEMPERATURE		
degrees Fahrenheit	0.56 (*after* subtracting 32)	degrees Celsius

Built during the seventh century after the Arab conquest of Jerusalem, the eight-sided Dome of the Rock stands on the Temple Mount, an area sacred to both Jews and Muslims. Originally the site of the ancient Jewish temple built by King Solomon, the Dome of the Rock is an Islamic shrine honoring the place from which the Muslim prophet Muhammad is believed to have ascended to heaven.

Introduction

In the past few decades, perhaps no country has been in the news more often or has captured international attention more frequently than Israel. The nation has become prominent because it lies at the center of the most persistent conflict in the Middle East.

Modern Israel is in part a product of an international movement called Zionism. The Zionist movement was established in the nineteenth century by Jews who sought to create a Jewish national or religious homeland in Palestine—a region of the Middle East that is revered as the Holy Land by Jews, Christians, and Muslims (followers of the Islamic religion).

One reason for the new home was to provide a refuge from the discrimination that Jews had encountered throughout the history of Western civilization. When the United Nations divided Palestine into Jewish and Arab territories in November 1947, it set in motion the process that led to the Declaration of Independence by Israel on May 14, 1948.

That declaration, in turn, led to an attack on Israel by its surrounding Arab neighbors. Israel won the resulting war, and about 700,000 Palestinian Arabs fled their homeland, becoming refugees in nearby countries. The political struggle that resulted continues to affect countries throughout the world as well as in the Middle East. During its short history, Israel has been portrayed both as an underdog fighting for survival and as a small state with too much firepower compared to its neighbors.

Israel actually has two histories, bridged by nearly 2,000 years of Jewish exile from Palestine. The ancient history of Israel has been recorded in sources such as the Old Testament of the Bible. The kingdom of David and Solomon was established around the year 1000 B.C. Jews resided in the region until about A.D. 70, when their rebellion against the imperial Roman government failed.

As a result, the Romans exiled the Jews, scattering them into various parts of the Roman Empire—Egypt, Morocco, Spain, northern Europe, and even Rome itself—an action referred to as the Diaspora (dispersal). The Holy Temple in Jerusalem, the center of religious life and the focal point of national unity for the Jews, was destroyed, and Israel was renamed Syria Palestina.

Palestine remained under Roman rule until the Arabs conquered the area in A.D. 635. The Arabs held it, except for a brief period during the twelfth century, until 1258. After the thirteenth century, the region of Palestine was ruled by various groups—most notably the Ottoman Turks, who were in control from 1517 until near the end of World War I. The end of the Ottoman Empire after the First World War created the opportunity for Zionist activity that brought about a Jewish nation in 1948.

Since 1948 two preoccupations have dominated Israel's existence. First, the new nation has been searching for security because of persistent armed conflict with the Arabs. Second, the Jews have worked to reestablish their presence in a place they had been largely absent from for 1,900 years. Many Jews view modern Israel as a fulfillment of biblical prophecy, and, as a result, Israel considers itself unique among nations.

Courtesy of Munir Nasr/UNRWA

After the formation of Israel in 1948 and the ensuing Arab-Israeli wars, many Palestinian Arabs who had lived in Palestine for hundreds of years fled the region to escape the dangers of the conflict. The United Nations Relief and Works Agency (UNRWA) set up camps, where the refugees live in overcrowded conditions.

For centuries, shepherds have tended their flocks along the shores of the Sea of Galilee. The Jews call this freshwater lake the Sea of Kinneret, from the Hebrew word *kinnor,* which means violin—an apt description of the curving lakeshore.

1) The Land

The State of Israel is a small country in southwestern Asia, or the Middle East, that covers an area of 7,992 square miles, roughly the size of the state of New Jersey. Measuring 265 miles from north to south and about 10 to 70 miles from west to east, the country is half desert. Israel's neighbors are Lebanon to the north, Syria and Jordan to the east, and Egypt to the southwest. Along the west Israel is bounded by the Mediterranean Sea.

Throughout its recent history, Israel has sought to increase national security by extending its borders. Thus, the ownership of some lands outside these boundaries is disputed between Israel and its neighbors. These areas include the Gaza Strip along the Mediterranean, the West Bank of the Jordan River, and the Golan Heights on Israel's northeastern border with Syria.

Topography

Geographically, Israel can be divided into three belts from west to east. The westernmost area, along the Mediterranean, is the coastal plain, with sandy beaches, sand dunes, and low hills. The center belt is a hilly region that comprises, from north to south, the hills of Galilee,

7

The Plain of Esdraelon—seen here from Mount Tabor in northeastern Israel—was swampland before 1920. In the 1920s and 1930s it was drained to create fertile farms.

The Negev Desert is the site not only of large irrigation schemes but also of this vast nature reserve, Ein Avdat, which lines the bottom of a wadi, or streambed. It is one of over 250 reserves developed in Israel after the Nature Reserves Authority was created in 1964.

the hills of Samaria, the Judaean hills, and the craggy hills of the Negev Desert. Most of Samaria and Judaea lie within the Israeli-occupied West Bank—the section west of the Jordan River that is claimed by both the Palestinian Arabs and Israel.

The Negev Desert in the south was once about 20 percent larger in area. At one time the desert began just south of the cities of Tel Aviv–Jaffa along the coast and Rehovot in the central region. Now it has been pushed back by agricultural development as far as Beersheba. Both in the

Negev and in the adjoining broad valley known as Wadi al-Araba, kibbutzim and moshavim—agricultural settlements that produce grain, corn, melons, alfalfa, and

The sands of isolated desert areas choke out many forms of vegetation.

The Dead Sea is a saltwater lake, and its heavy concentrations of minerals congeal into crusty, solid formations. Although the Dead Sea receives fresh water from the Jordan River and other, smaller streams, it has no outlet of its own. Only evaporation, aided by the hot desert climate, carries off the lake's inflow.

citrus products—have been established. Israelis are working to extend agriculture south all the way to the Gulf of Aqaba.

The easternmost topographical belt is known as the Jordan Rift—part of the larger Great Rift Valley. This deep depression in the earth was formed millions of years ago by the sinking of the earth's crust, during which the floor of the Jordan River Valley and the Dead Sea collapsed to 1,300 feet below sea level and mountains rose up on either side. The fault line begins in northern Syria, travels down through the Jordan River Valley, the Red Sea, and East Africa, ending in Mozambique in southeastern Africa.

Because of the dry, hot climate of the Great Rift Valley, many ancient biblical manuscripts have been preserved in hillside caves. The Dead Sea Scrolls, for example—which were discovered at Khirbat Qumran on the West Bank—contain many ancient manuscripts, some of which are the oldest handwritten copies of the Old Testament. They are now on display in Jerusalem at the Shrine of the Book.

Rivers and Seas

The most important river in Israel is the Jordan, which rises in the Golan Heights, runs southward through the Sea of Galilee, and ends at the Dead Sea. Through a national pipeline system that emerges from the Sea of Galilee—a freshwater body—

The strong currents of the Jordan River are used to power hydroelectric stations in Israel, which makes the river a valuable energy resource.

9

Courtesy of Minneapolis Public Library and Information Center

In 1947 Bedouin—wandering Arabs—discovered eight ancient manuscripts in the caves at Khirbat Qumran. Archaeological digs revealed additional documents that have become known as the Dead Sea Scrolls. Evidently the literature of a Jewish brotherhood, the scrolls are believed to have been written between about 200 B.C. and A.D. 68.

water from the Jordan is carried south as far as Beersheba and is used for drinking as well as for irrigation.

At approximately 1,300 feet below sea level, Israel's Dead Sea has the lowest elevation on earth. With water that is about three times as salty as the Mediterranean, the Dead Sea has such a high mineral content that it cannot sustain life, making it literally "dead."

In recent years, portions of the Dead Sea have dried up, partly because some of the Jordan's waters have been diverted to irrigate desert lands. Furthermore, mining operations intentionally speed up evaporation of the Dead Sea to make it easier to extract minerals. The Dead Sea contains an estimated 1,000 million tons of magnesium chloride, magnesium bromide, and sodium chloride (salt) and is one of the world's greatest single sources of potash, which is used in fertilizers.

Other rivers in Israel are much smaller. The Yarqon flows from the hills east of Tel Aviv–Jaffa on a 16-mile course to the sea. Although this river has little significance economically, it offers leisure attractions to the inhabitants of Tel Aviv–Jaffa. In addition, the Qarn, Qishon, and Hadera rivers water northern Israel, and the Besor flows south of Beersheba during part of the year.

Israel has many other waterways, but they are dry most of the year. These streambeds, called wadis, are found in the Negev Desert. During the winter rainy season, even relatively small amounts of rainfall can cause flash flooding because the ground cannot absorb much moisture. As a result, a dry piece of desert can become a raging wall of water shortly after a storm. The Bedouin Arabs who live in the Negev Desert know the perils of such rainfall. During the dry summers, they live in the wadis with their families and animals. During the winter, however, they pack up their tents and move to the relative safety of the hills.

In the Middle East, water is a very precious commodity. Whoever controls water in the region controls life. Many disputes have arisen over water rights, and the search for new water sources continues. Recently, a huge underground reservoir of water was discovered thousands of feet below the surface of the Negev Desert. Israeli scientists are now researching ways to purify salt water for agricultural use.

Flora and Fauna

From midwinter to spring Israel's hillsides and valleys come alive with wildflowers. The blooming plants include red anemones, white cyclamen, scarlet poppies, wild tulips, roses, and fields of sunflowers. Some 2,500 species of plants grow in Israel, including the sabra, or cactus, which is the name given to native-born

The sabra—an Arabic word that means "prickly pear"—yields a pulpy, edible fruit.

Israelis, for, like the cactus, they are said to be prickly on the outside but soft and sweet within.

Almond trees around the Sea of Galilee burst into white blossoms in January. Trees that bear fruit—such as figs, olives, dates, and pomegranates—are successfully cultivated. Eucalyptus trees, imported from Australia, are scattered throughout the land. Because the eucalyptus grows rapidly and has a well-developed root system, it helps to keep desert sands from creeping into new areas.

During winter, masses of birds fleeing from colder climates converge on Israel. Waterfowl—such as pelicans, egrets, purple herons, and storks—as well as mountain and desert birds find refuge in Israel's Mediterranean weather. Migratory birds and the local, year-round varieties together represent about 350 different species.

Reptiles—such as lizards and snakes—populate the Dead Sea Basin and the Negev. Although the waters of the Dead Sea are too salty for aquatic life, the Sea of Galilee and the Mediterranean support fish, and carp are raised in artificial ponds. Concentrated in the fertile Jordan River Valley and along the shores of the Dead Sea are wildcats, hyenas, jackals, foxes,

Courtesy of Steve Feinstein

Wildflowers dot Israel's landscape.

Courtesy of Steve Feinstein

A vividly colored fish swims along coral reefs in the waters at Eilat, Israel's outlet to the Red Sea.

wolves, boars, and gazelles. Hunting is prohibited, and the government has set up several game preserves.

Climate

Israel has a Mediterranean climate, with long, hot, dry summers and short, cool, rainy winters. The climatic pattern, however, varies from one region to the next because of differences in altitude and in distance from the sea. In August, Israel's hottest month, temperatures average 75° F in northern Galilee and 90° F in the Rift Valley. Temperatures may, however, rise above 125° F in the Rift Valley because of its low elevation and long distance from the Mediterranean. During the coolest month of January, temperatures range from 45° F in northern Galilee to 60° F in the Rift Valley. Water may freeze in the hilly areas a few days each winter.

Spoonbills and pelicans gather on Lake Hula, part of a nature reserve located north of Galilee.

Independent Picture Service

Most of Israel's rain falls between the months of November and April. Snow occasionally covers the hills of the northern and central regions. Northern Galilee averages about 40 inches of precipitation each year—the highest in the country. Eilat at the southern tip of the Negev, on the other hand, receives an average of only one inch of rain each year. During the spring and fall, hot, dry winds—called khamsins—sometimes enter Israel from the deserts to the east. The dust and sand often carried by these winds can impair visibility, and the humidity can drop to an uncomfortable zero percent.

Cities

About 85 percent of Israel's people live in cities and towns. Jerusalem, which Israel declared as its capital in 1949, is the nation's largest city, with a population of

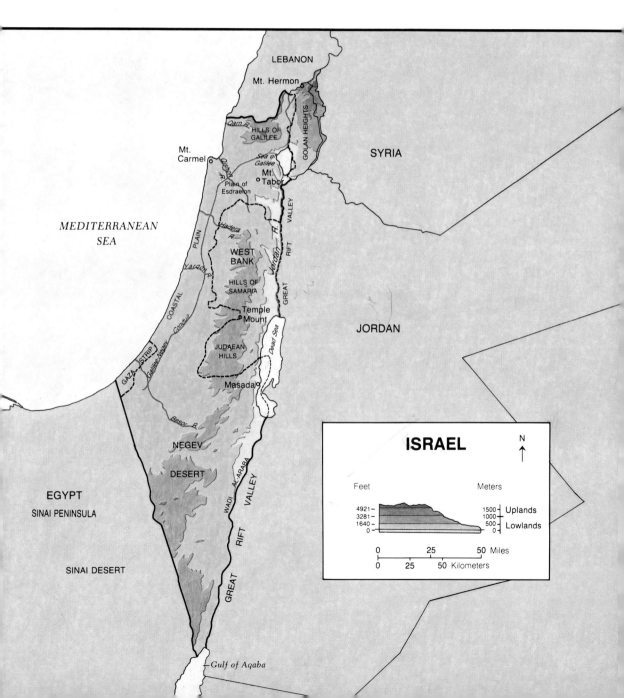

Jerusalem's Old City is viewed from the top of the Lutheran Church of the Redeemer.

the Old City in the eastern half and the Israelis controlled the new city in the western portion. Israeli forces occupied the Jordanian section during the Six-Day War in 1967 and have since integrated it with the newer, Jewish sector. Jerusalem has expanded into areas that are part of Israel, as well as into the Israeli-occupied West Bank. Many Israelis are attracted to Jerusalem because of its biblical heritage.

Only 40 miles from Jerusalem, Tel Aviv–Jaffa is Israel's second largest city, with a population of 328,000. The entire metropolitan area of Tel Aviv–Jaffa, however, has a population of more than 1.3 million people. It is the industrial center of Israel, as well as the center for textile trade and diamond exchange. Because foreign countries do not recognize Israel's claim to both the old and new sections of Jerusalem, they maintain their embassies in Tel Aviv.

Built along the slopes of Mount Carmel, the city of Haifa, with a population of 235,000, is Israel's third largest urban area as well as a major port. Beersheba is the capital of the Negev region and has a population of 110,000.

430,000, including both the old and new, or eastern and western, sections of the city. Jerusalem was designated as an international zone in the partition of Palestine proposed by the United Nations in 1947. In 1948 during the first Arab-Israeli war, however, Jordanian Arabs took over

Festive lights adorn Kings of Israel Square in Tel Aviv-Jaffa. Crowning the square is the modern City Hall.

Haifa stretches along the coast of the Mediterranean Sea. The city probably derives its name from two Hebrew words, *hof yaffe,* which mean "beautiful coast."

Since the 1950s Israel has sought to distribute its population more evenly between large cities and newly developed towns. Between 1950 and 1962, the immigration of more than 500,000 Jews from Arab countries in North Africa and the Middle East spurred relocation efforts. The immigrants settled in development towns, where inexpensive apartments, land for industrial development, and loans were available. Model towns, such as Carmiel, have grown to between 12,000 and 22,000 people. Some of the towns, however, like Bet She'an (population 12,900) and Yeroham (population 6,200), lack a strong economic base and have not done as well.

Beersheba has experienced rapid residential and industrial development since 1948. This recent shift into a more modern era contrasts with its ancient heritage, which spans about 4,000 years.

A model of the city and the Second Temple restored by King Herod recreates the Jewish community in Jerusalem during the first century B.C.

2) History and Government

The Jewish presence in what is now Israel began around 1800 B.C., when a shepherd named Abraham led a group of people across the Euphrates River from Mesopotamia (Iraq and northeastern Syria) and wandered into Canaan, as Palestine was called then. Leading a nomadic life, Abraham and his people set up tents and dug seven wells at one point and, according to legend, named the site Beersheba, which means seven wells.

The Land of Canaan

The Canaanites called the newcomers *Ibriim* (Hebrews), which in their language meant "the people who crossed over" or "the people from the other side of the riv-

er." Nomads without a territory of their own, the Hebrews continued to wander within the land of Canaan until a famine struck the area in the early fifteenth century B.C.

The Hebrews then migrated into Egypt, where after a time they were enslaved by the Egyptians. During the thirteenth century B.C., a prophet named Moses led the Hebrews out of Egyptian bondage. Many years later Moses' successor, Joshua, conquered parts of Canaan, and the Hebrews began to lead a settled lifestyle. Unlike other people in the region, who worshipped many deities, the Hebrews believed that there was only one God.

For about 200 years the Hebrews—united as a confederation of tribes called the Israelites—fought various peoples in Canaan. Their strongest enemies were the Philistines, who controlled Philistia on the southwestern coast of Canaan. Although the Israelites defeated the Canaanites by about 1125 B.C., their struggles with the Philistines continued. With superior weapons and better military organization, the Philistines defeated the Israelites in about 1050 B.C.

The Philistine victory forced the Israelites to band together more tightly than they had done before. They united under a monarchy and chose Saul as their king. Saul's successor, David, defeated the Philistines around 1000 B.C. and established Jerusalem as the capital of the kingdom of Israel. Upon the death of Solomon, David's son and successor, feuding Hebrew tribes split the kingdom into Israel in the north and Judah in the south. Citizens

Abraham's Well is said to be one of the original seven wells dug by Abraham, leader of the Hebrews.

came to be known as Jews—a variation of the Hebrew term *Yehudi*, which means "citizen of Judah."

Invasions and Conquests

In 721 B.C. the Assyrians—who were extending their rule westward from present-day Iraq—conquered Israel. The southern kingdom of Judah, however, continued to exist until 586 B.C., when the Babylonians —who succeeded the Assyrians as the dominant power in the region—destroyed Jerusalem and exiled many Jews. But the Jews did not forget Jerusalem, and about 50 years later, when Cyrus the Great of Persia conquered the Babylonians, he permitted the Jews to return to their former capital and rebuild the city.

The Persian Empire fell to the Greeks under Alexander the Great in 331 B.C. Alexander, like the Persian rulers before him, respected the Jewish belief in one God and granted Jews religious freedom as well as a considerable amount of self-government. After Alexander's death his successors—the Ptolemies of Egypt and the Seleucids of Syria—controlled the region.

Eventually, Greek rule became oppressive to the Jews when the Seleucids tried

In this seventeenth-century Dutch painting, artist Rembrandt van Rijn depicts the Hebrew patriarch Jacob wrestling with an angel of God. According to tradition, when Jacob fought the angel, God gave him the name Israel, meaning "he who struggled with God." Thereafter, the Hebrews became known as Israelites.

Solomon's Pillars in the Negev Desert are thought to mark the site where King Solomon exploited extensive copper mines.

to impose their culture and religion on the population. Under the leadership of the Maccabees, the Jews revolted and set up an independent state in 141 B.C. The Jewish state lasted less than a century, however, until Pompey the Great conquered Judah for the Roman Empire in 63 B.C. and renamed the country Judaea.

Roman Rule

Conflicts arose between the Roman rulers and those Jews who wanted to retain their religious practices and govern themselves. These religious Jews—known as Zealots—rebelled against Rome in A.D. 66. Although thousands of Jews died in the four-year war that followed and Jerusalem was nearly destroyed, several Jewish settlements survived.

In A.D. 132 Simon Bar Kokhba led Jewish fighters in a final effort to overthrow the Roman yoke. After three years of war, however, the Romans broke Jewish resistance. Determined that the Jews would never again rebel, the Roman emperor Hadrian drove the Jews from their

The Roman amphitheater at Caesarea, the Roman capital of Palestine, was built during Herod's reign. Now completely restored, the 20,000-seat theater is the site of an annual summer music festival.

Courtesy of Steve Feinstein

Both Muslims and Jews pray at this site, where a mosque was constructed over the Cave of Machpelah in Hebron on the West Bank. Abraham, considered the father of both religions, purchased the cave to bury his wife, Sarah. The place has since become known as the Tomb of the Patriarchs, because Abraham, Isaac, Jacob, and their respective wives are believed to be buried within the chamber.

homeland. Judaea was renamed Palestine, which was derived from the word "Philistine," and Jerusalem became known as Aelia Capitolina.

This scattering of the Jews, the Jewish Diaspora, would last for approximately 1,900 years. First in the Mediterranean area and later in northern Europe and points east, the Jews wandered throughout the world. Often the victims of discrimination that had cultural and religious roots, the Jews nevertheless clung to their faith, their customs, and their history—and to the hope of returning one day to their homeland.

For the next 500 years, Palestine remained in Roman hands. First it was part of the Roman Empire, and, after the fourth century A.D., it belonged to the Eastern Roman, or Byzantine, Empire.

During this period the religion of Christianity grew around its founder, Jesus of Nazareth. Born a Jew and considered by his followers to be the long-awaited He-

brew Savior, Jesus gained many followers within and beyond the Jewish community. In A.D. 313 Constantine the Great, emperor of Rome, legalized Christianity. Eventually, he himself would be baptized a Christian.

Arab Control

In A.D. 637 the armies of the Arabs—who followed the Islamic faith—conquered Palestine, Egypt, and Syria. This was an important event for many reasons. First, it meant that a new people moved into the region with their own cultural contributions. Second, because Jerusalem held religious importance for the Muslims, it became a renewed city. Third, Arabs and Jews had a shared ancestry because both groups considered the prophet Abraham to be their father.

Arab control of the Middle East was beneficial to the Jews. Under Arab rule, Jews and Christians were given the status

19

Site of the last stand made by Jewish Zealots in their revolt against Roman rule (A.D. 66–73), Masada is a flat-topped hill at the southern end of the Dead Sea on which two fortified palaces were built during Herod's reign. When Jerusalem was captured by the Romans in A.D. 70, about 1,000 Jewish men, women, and children retreated to Masada (Hebrew for "fortress") where they withstood a two-year siege. In A.D. 73 the Zealots committed mass suicide rather than submit to their conquerors. The hill has since become a symbol of Jewish determination.

The shofar, or ram's horn, was used by ancient Hebrews in high religious observances and as a signal in battle. Shofars are still blown at the New Year (Rosh Hashana), and at the end of Yom Kippur (the Day of Atonement).

of dhimmis, or tolerated minorities, and were protected by the Arabs. During the golden age of Islam that followed, Jews benefited from the rich economic and cultural foundations introduced by the Arab rulers. Although the Arab center of power was in Damascus and later Baghdad, Jerusalem became an important city for the Arabs.

Palestine was also important for Christians, since the life and ministry of Jesus of Nazareth took place in Judaea. Many

Europeans viewed the region as historically part of the Roman Empire and thus part of Christian lands. In 1095 Pope Urban II called on the knights of Europe to begin a crusade to recapture the Holy Land—which included Jerusalem, Palestine, and Syria—for Christianity. The crusaders had some initial success, capturing Jerusalem in 1099. Their victories in Palestine, however, failed to establish a permanent presence, and their short-lived kingdom of Jerusalem collapsed in 1187.

The Arabs regained control of the region until 1258, when the Mongols from eastern Asia destroyed Baghdad and ended direct Arab political control. The Mamluks—a group of rulers who had originally been brought to the region from central Asia to

Ruins of the crusader fortress at Atlit—a reminder of the European invasions during the Middle Ages—rise along the Mediterranean shore.

Mosaic floors from the sixth-century synagogue of Bet Alfa depict the signs of the zodiac—the 12 constellations used in astrology—and symbols of the four seasons.

serve as slaves—controlled Palestine from the mid-thirteenth century until 1517. In that year the Ottoman Turks, who had moved into the Middle East from eastern Asia, embraced Islam and conquered the area of Palestine from the Mamluks. Palestine was an administrative district within the Ottoman Empire until the Turks were forced to give up their Arab possessions after World War I.

The Growth of Zionism

During the nineteenth century the Zionist movement developed in Europe. The movement, which was stimulated by the oppression of Jews in eastern Europe, set as its goal the return of the Jewish people to Palestine. In 1897 Theodor Herzl, author of *The Jewish State,* founded the World Zionist Organization to carry out the plan. Although the Ottoman Turks rejected

Zionism because of Arab resistance, the Zionists bought land in the early twentieth century and established farm settlements in Palestine. By 1911 Arabs in Palestine had organized opposition to the influx of Jews.

The leaders of the World Zionist Organization failed to negotiate land agreements with the native Arab population, although a dialogue on the issue of Jewish settlement continued through the 1920s. Thus, the seeds of conflict between Arabs and Jews were sown. Zionists viewed Palestine as the solution to the Jewish problem. But the Arabs also had a claim to the land, and they were not enthusiastic about large-scale Jewish immigration to Palestine.

World War I

By the outset of World War I in 1914, the Arabs also desired independence for

A tiny Greek Orthodox church stands at Capernaum. Located on the northwestern shore of the Sea of Galilee, this Palestinian city, which is now in ruins, is believed to have been the home of Jesus during most of his adult life.

Resting on a marble base, the top outer walls of the Dome of the Rock are formed by a series of elaborately decorated windows and mosaic ceramic panels. Worked into the patterns both inside and outside the shrine are Arabic inscriptions, some of which quote the Koran (the book of Islamic sacred writings).

Courtesy of Steve Feinstein

themselves. They saw the decline of the Ottoman Empire as an opportunity to assert their own authority in their homeland, but they feared the outside threat of Zionist interest in the region. When Britain promised the Arabs independence after the war, the Arabs decided to support the British in the global conflict. The agreement established in the British MacMahon letters of 1915, however, did not clarify whether Palestine would be included in this Arab territory.

Meanwhile, in 1916 Britain and France concluded the Sykes-Picot Agreement, which stated that Palestine, Syria, and Iraq would be divided between the two European countries. In a third, conflicting commitment—the Balfour Declaration of 1917—Britain promised the Jews, whose help it wanted in the war effort, a Jewish "national home" in Palestine.

Thus, when the British mandate over Palestine was established in 1920, the British felt obligated to help create a Jewish national home as well as to ensure Arab independence. It was not clear, however, if the word "homeland" meant "state." Nevertheless, after 1922 the borders of Palestine were established, with the Mediterranean bordering the west, the Jordan River and the Great Rift Valley lying to the east, Lebanon forming the northern

boundary, and the Sinai Desert marking the southern frontier. No more than 15,000 Jews per year were allowed to immigrate to Palestine from other parts of the world.

Arab Uprisings

Although the Balfour Declaration advocated the establishment of a Jewish homeland in Palestine, it emphasized that a return of the Jews should not negatively

Independent Picture Service

A seven-branched menorah, or candelabrum, was used in ancient rituals held in King Solomon's temple. Variations on this object have come to symbolize the Jewish heritage.

23

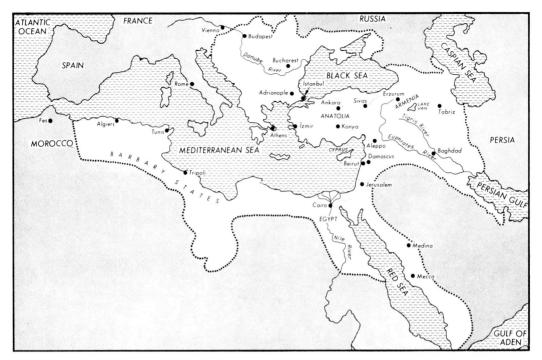

Ottoman power reached its peak in the sixteenth century under the rule of Suleyman I. At this time, social and governmental institutions that had been evolving for many years became strict codes of law. These laws were to last for four centuries. By the middle of the seventeenth century, the vast Ottoman Empire included all of the Middle East, much of North Africa, and most of Eastern Europe. Under Ottoman rule, Arab lands were severely neglected. Map taken from *The Area Handbook for the Republic of Turkey,* 1973.

affect the native Arab population. Nevertheless, as Jewish immigration to Palestine increased during the 1920s and as Arabs consequently lost control over some of their lands, rioting broke out.

Jewish immigration rose sharply when the anti-Jewish Nazis came to power in Germany in 1933. Fearful of Jewish domination, the Palestinian Arabs revolted against British control from 1936 to 1939. They rejected several compromise proposals set forth by the British. In 1939 Britain again limited the yearly quota of Jews who could immigrate to Palestine in a white paper, or official statement.

The Post–World-War-II Era

The horrors of the Holocaust—in which six million Jews were killed by the Nazis—evoked world sympathy for European Jews and the Zionist cause. Nevertheless, Britain continued to limit Jewish immigration into Palestine. Survivors of the death camps had no homes to go to, and many found their way to Palestine illegally.

Meanwhile, tension between Jews and Arabs within Palestine continued to intensify. In 1947 Britain declared the mandate that had been established after World War I unworkable and asked the United Nations (UN) to help solve the Palestinian problem. The UN Special Commission on Palestine recommended that Palestine be divided into an Arab state and a Jewish state, with Jerusalem put under international control. Zionists were pleased with the plan—finally the world had recognized their right to a state in Palestine. The Arabs, on the other hand, refused to accept any partition plan and felt all the more abused by the fact that the Jewish

On the grounds at Yad Vashem, the museum of the Holocaust, this sculpture commemorates victims of the Nazi concentration camps.

Courtesy of Embassy of Israel

minority was to receive 55 percent of the land.

The Palestine War

In accordance with the UN resolution, Britain withdrew from Palestine on May 14, 1948, and on the same day the Jewish people proclaimed the independent state of Israel. The Arab states of Egypt, Jordan, Syria, Lebanon, Iraq, Saudi Arabia,

Independent Picture Service

Chaim Weizmann, scientist and president of the World Zionist Organization after Theodor Herzl's death, served as the first president of the new nation of Israel.

and the Yemens promptly declared war against Israel, beginning a conflict known as the Palestine War or—to the Jews—as the War of Independence. The surrounding nations outnumbered the Jews in population 40 to 1 and in area 400 to 1. To face the combined enemy armies, including Jordan's famed Arab Legion, the Jews had about 35,000 trained *Haganah* (military defense) troops.

To further complicate Israel's position, the state was bordered on three sides by enemy nations. Not only was it impossible to patrol the borders adequately, but Israel was only 10 miles wide in places, making the new nation vulnerable and leaving it no place to which it could retreat. The Arabs initially gained the upper hand, but when the Jews broke the Arab siege of Jerusalem, the tide of the war began to turn.

When the fighting ended, Israel held about half of the area that the UN had planned for a new Arab state, in addition to the territory intended for Israel. Egypt and Jordan held the rest of Palestine, and the city of Jerusalem was split between Jordan and Israel. For the Jewish people

25

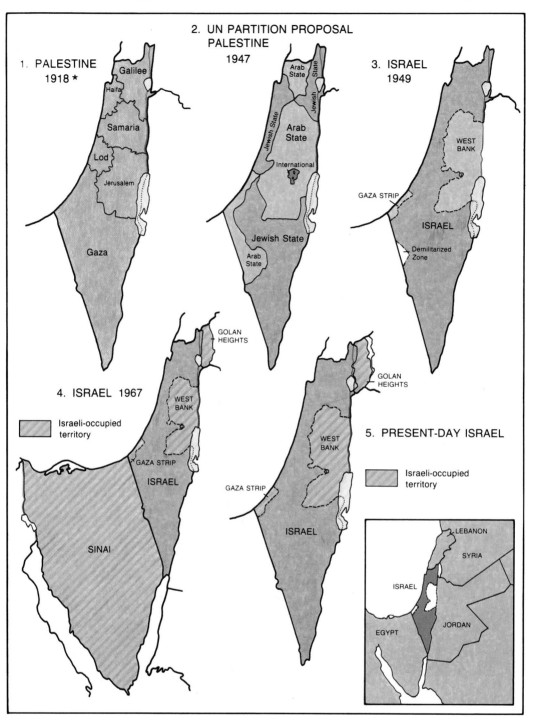

1. PALESTINE 1918 *

Galilee
Haifa
Samaria
Lod
Jerusalem
Gaza

2. UN PARTITION PROPOSAL PALESTINE 1947

Arab State
Jewish State
Jewish State
Arab State
International
Jewish State
Arab State

3. ISRAEL 1949

WEST BANK
GAZA STRIP
ISRAEL
Demilitarized Zone

4. ISRAEL 1967

GOLAN HEIGHTS
Israeli-occupied territory
WEST BANK
GAZA STRIP
ISRAEL
SINAI

5. PRESENT-DAY ISRAEL

GOLAN HEIGHTS
WEST BANK
GAZA STRIP
Israeli-occupied territory
ISRAEL
LEBANON
SYRIA
ISRAEL
EGYPT
JORDAN

Artwork by Carol F. Barrett

These maps depict the changing boundaries of Palestine and Israel during the twentieth century. MAP 1 shows the boundaries and internal districts of Palestine under British rule in 1918. MAP 2 outlines the UN's proposal in 1947 to partition Palestine into a Jewish state, an Arab state, and an international zone to be administered by the UN. The cities of Jerusalem and Bethlehem lie within the international zone. MAP 3 shows Israel after the first Arab-Israeli war, with the armistice lines *(dashed)* established in 1949 around the West Bank and the Gaza Strip. Jordan annexed the West Bank after this war, and Egypt claimed the Gaza Strip as a protectorate. MAP 4 illustrates the post–Six-Day-War areas occupied by Israel in 1967: the Sinai Peninsula, the Gaza Strip, the West Bank, and the Golan Heights. MAP 5 depicts the present boundaries of Israel and of Israeli-occupied territory. (Israel returned the Sinai Peninsula to Egypt after the peace treaty of 1979.)

*Excluding areas east of the Jordan River.

Courtesy of Steve Feinstein

the Diaspora had ended, but for the Palestinian Arabs it had just begun. Many Palestinian Arabs left their lands in 1948 to escape the fighting. In some cases, the Israelis evicted Arabs who occupied important strategic positions. Within the first three months of Israel's creation, over 700,000 Arabs left the country, and only 160,000 remained.

The Arab nations promptly imposed a strict economic boycott and cut off all communications with Israel. Although

Courtesy of Steve Feinstein

Huge refugee camps have been set up by the UNRWA on the West Bank and in Jordan to aid displaced Palestinians. Some refugees have left the camps and have become integrated into the life of neighboring Arab countries or of the Western world. Others remain in the camps, determined to return to their original homeland.

27

David Ben-Gurion, one of Israel's founding fathers, reads the new nation's Declaration of Independence. On the wall above him is a portrait of Theodor Herzl.

dangerous border raids by Arab guerrilla fighters continued, Israel was no longer at war, and it could turn its attention to internal development. The new nation held its first election in January 1949. The Knesset (parliament) named Chaim Weizmann president. Weizmann appointed David Ben-Gurion—who would have a strong influence on Israel's development—as the prime minister. But peace was not to last. Several military encounters were to follow in the years to come.

The Suez-Sinai War

Border clashes increased between Arab and Israeli guerrilla fighters, especially along the frontier with Egypt. On October

Egyptian guns dominated the entrance to the Gulf of Aqaba before the outbreak of the Six-Day War in 1967.

Israelis gained control of Jerusalem's Western Wall in June 1967.

Independent Picture Service

29, 1956, Israel launched a military campaign against Egyptian bases in Sinai. Israel's army crossed the Sinai Desert, knocking out one-third of the Egyptian regular army and destroying Arab military bases. Within a few days the Israeli army reached the Suez Canal. Israeli forces withdrew by early 1957, and UN peacekeeping forces replaced them along the Negev-Sinai border and in the Gaza Strip.

The Six-Day War

Clashes along Israel's borders with Syria and Jordan escalated in the mid-1960s. Egypt demanded removal of the UN forces from Sinai and the Gaza Strip. The UN complied, and the Egyptian army entered Sinai and blockaded the Strait of Tiran, halting Israel's vital trade with the East. Israel mobilized its forces and on June 5, 1967, simultaneously attacked Egypt, Jordan, and Syria.

The Arab air forces were destroyed before they could leave their air bases. Israeli ground forces swept halfway to Damascus in Syria and all the way to the Suez Canal. After just six days of fighting, a cease-fire was declared. Israel held the Sinai Peninsula, the West Bank of the Jordan River,

Courtesy of Israel Government Press Office

Israeli troops were able to trap and defeat the retreating Egyptian army at Mitla Pass on the Sinai Peninsula after the Israeli air force took control of the air during the Six-Day War.

Courtesy of Steve Feinstein

The Tel Fahr memorial in the Golan Heights commemorates Israeli soldiers killed while taking the ridges in June 1967.

and some strategic ridges known as the Golan Heights within Syria. Israel's lasting possession of these lands, however, remained in doubt.

The Palestine Liberation Organization (PLO)

After 1967 a new force—Palestinian guerrilla fighters—presented itself in the conflict. Led by the Palestine Liberation Organization (PLO), a group formed in the Gaza Strip in 1964, Palestinian Arabs decided to take forceful initiatives of their own to liberate their former home. Border violations again intensified, and guerrilla groups struck both at Israel and at Jews around the world. The main target of Arab attack was commercial aviation, and numerous airplanes were hijacked to the Mid-

Courtesy of UNRWA

This no-man's-land—an uninhabited area—in Jerusalem was patrolled by Jordan from 1948 to 1967.

30

dle East during the late 1960s and early 1970s. Such acts of violence concerned not only Israel but also the United States, West Germany, Greece, Switzerland, Great Britain, and even neighboring Arab states that were hostile to Israel.

Yasir Arafat has been an active leader of the Palestinians. In 1956 he formed the organization Al-Fatah, which later became part of the Palestine Liberation Organization (PLO). In 1968 Arafat was named chairman of the PLO, becoming a chief organizer of PLO guerrilla activities. Driven from Jordan in 1970, from Lebanon in 1982, and from Syria in 1983, Arafat has since lost the confidence of many of his followers.

In 1973 crowds gather for a huge parade, complete with army tanks, to celebrate the twenty-fifth anniversary of Israel's independence.

The Yom Kippur War

In October 1973 on Yom Kippur, the holiest day of the Jewish religious year, the armies of Syria and Egypt attacked Israel to regain the territories they had lost in 1967. The Israelis were caught off guard, just as the Arabs had been in the Six-Day War. Fierce aerial battles took place in the skies over Israel, and Egyptian ground forces crossed the Suez Canal into the Sinai Peninsula.

Egypt and Syria were backed by the oil-rich nations of Saudi Arabia and Kuwait, which provided funding for the most sophisticated Soviet weapons. When the Western world came to Israel's aid, Saudi Arabia and Kuwait, which supplied most of the world's oil, cut off petroleum exports to nations that supported Israel in any way.

To avoid a showdown, the United States and the Soviet Union intervened and mediated a cease-fire arrangement. With U.S. secretary of state Henry Kissinger acting as mediator, Egypt and Syria signed agree-

Independent Picture Service

During the Yom Kippur War of 1973, Israeli troops raised their nation's flag over Mount Hermon, which, at 9,232 feet above sea level, is the highest peak in the mountain range between Lebanon and Syria.

Courtesy of Embassy of Arab Republic of Egypt

In 1973 Egyptian soldiers stormed across the Suez Canal to attack the Israeli Bar-Lev line, which had been built to provide shelter for Israeli defense troops. The surprise attack occurred on Yom Kippur, the holiest day of the Jewish religious year.

ments with Israel in 1974 that arranged for the exchange of prisoners and that established cease-fire lines.

Obstacles to Peace

The accord, however, did not resolve two of the most important obstacles to peace in the Middle East—the fate of the territories seized by Israel in the Six-Day War of 1967 and the future of the Palestinian Arabs. The two questions are closely interrelated, because a future Palestinian homeland could require that Israel give up part of the West Bank.

Most Israelis object to the Arab demand that Israel retreat to the pre-1967 borders and permit the existence of an independent Palestinian state. Such a state, they feel, would provide a launching pad for Arab guerrilla activities. Some Israelis are ready to make territorial compromises to secure peace and lasting security. Others, however, refuse to yield an inch of territory. Many Palestinians are equally inflexible in their demands.

The Camp David Meetings

In 1977 President Anwar el-Sadat of Egypt took the bold step of offering to meet with Israeli leaders in Jerusalem to negotiate peace and to settle the Palestinian issue. Although there was great enthusiasm for the Sadat visit, discussions between the two states made little progress. President Jimmy Carter of the United States intervened to help the peace process along by inviting Menachem Begin, the Israeli prime minister, and President Sadat to meet at Camp David, Maryland, in September 1978.

The Camp David meetings led to a peace treaty between Egypt and Israel that called for Israel to withdraw from the Sinai Peninsula in several phases. In return, Egypt recognized the existence of Israel. The two countries established full diplomatic relations as well as economic

Independent Picture Service

Anwar el-Sadat, who became president of Egypt in 1970, steered his country's foreign policy toward improved relations with Israel and the West.

Courtesy of Nobel Foundation

Israeli leader Menachem Begin *(above)* and Anwar el-Sadat of Egypt were awarded the Nobel Prize for peace for their joint efforts to negotiate a peace treaty between the two nations.

33

Sadat *(left)* and Begin *(right)* shake hands at Camp David as U.S. president Jimmy Carter looks on. Although the settlement reached by the two men represented an important breakthrough in Arab-Israeli relations, some people maintain that the failure to resolve the issue of a homeland for the Palestinians was a major flaw in the agreement.

Courtesy of Jimmy Carter Library

agreements. In addition, travel between the two countries was resumed. The peace process begun at Camp David also called for a five-year transition period after which some undefined form of Palestinian Arab self-rule would be established on the West Bank and in the Gaza Strip. Although the peace treaty was signed on March 26, 1979, self-rule for Palestinians had not yet been achieved in 1988, and violence erupted between Israeli police and Palestinians in the occupied territories.

The Lebanon War

In the early 1970s a branch of the PLO took control of the southern part of Leb-

anon, a neighboring country torn by civil war. From southern Lebanon, the PLO launched guerrilla and rocket attacks on Israeli settlements. On June 6, 1982, Israel began an attack called "Operation Peace for Galilee" on the PLO in Lebanon. This operation sought to remove the PLO influence from southern Lebanon and to protect Israel's northern border. The Israelis pursued the Palestinians to the outskirts of the Lebanese capital of Beirut, besieging a large city that already had many complicated political problems. The Israelis hoped to help create a new political system in Lebanon led by the Maronite Christians, who the Israelis thought would sign a peace treaty with Israel.

During the Lebanese civil war of the late 1970s, Israel opened medical stations along its northern border to aid Lebanese civilians. The fence between the two countries has been named the "Good Fence."

Although the PLO was defeated and temporarily left Lebanon, Israel found itself embroiled in a renewed Lebanese civil war. Because Israel was a foreign power, most Lebanese factions tried to attack the Israeli forces and to push them out of the country. Within Israel, strong public opposition to Israeli involvement in Lebanon developed, and Israeli forces finally withdrew during the summer of 1985.

The Changing Domestic Scene

In the general election of May 18, 1977, the Labor party was defeated by Menachem Begin of the Likud (Unity) party. Many Israelis were startled by the outcome. The Labor party had been in power since Israel's foundation in 1948. It was the party of the pioneers, and many people identified it with the idealistic spirit of Israel's beginnings.

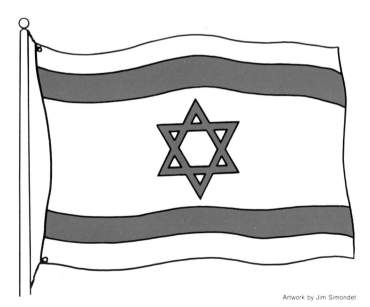

Inspired by the tallith, or Jewish prayer shawl, Zionists created the Israeli flag in the late nineteenth century. White and blue are the colors of the tallith, but they have also come to stand for Zionist ideals and for the sky, respectively. The six-pointed shield of David, a traditional Jewish symbol, fills the center of the flag.

35

The Labor party was defeated in part because many Israelis were dissatisfied with the nation's continuing economic crisis. Inflation increased sharply in 1977. The high cost of military defense caused taxes to rise. An even greater worry was that immigration—a cornerstone of the Israeli state—had declined sharply. The number of Israelis leaving the country began to equal the number of those entering it. Some Israelis were attracted by the more comfortable lifestyles available in other lands.

The Likud government gained a great deal of popularity, enhanced partly by the Camp David Agreement and the resulting peace with Egypt. Begin and the Likud party retained power in the 1981 elections, despite a strong challenge from the Labor party, which had aligned with other parties of the center-left.

With a mounting economic crisis, however, the Likud government lost much of its support, and both the Likud and Labor-Alignment parties received the same number of seats in the Israeli Knesset in the 1984 elections. Thus, neither party had sufficient votes to rule.

As a result, Yitzhak Shamir, successor to Menachem Begin in the Likud party,

and Shimon Peres, head of the Labor party, agreed to divide power. In a unique rotation agreement, Peres served as prime minister of the coalition government for the first two years, with Shamir as foreign minister, and in October 1986 they switched positions. The result was a fragile government coalition with intense rivalries between the parties and frequent threats from both parties of a call for new elections.

In Knesset elections held in November 1988, the Likud party gained a slight edge over Labor. Likud won in part because of the tough stand it takes on the Palestinian uprising that broke out in the occupied territories in late 1987. Whereas the Labor party is willing to give up some of the occupied lands to achieve real peace, Likud believes such an exchange would seriously endanger Israel's security.

The Government

Israel is a parliamentary democracy with the highest authority held by a unicameral (one-house) legislature called the Knesset. Although no constitution has been written, the Knesset enacts laws that regulate the government. The 120 Knesset mem-

The Knesset, or parliament, meets in this building, which was dedicated in 1966 and is part of a complex of government structures set among parks and gardens in Jerusalem.

Yitzhak Shamir, who leads the Likud party, became prime minister on October 20, 1986.

bers are elected to four-year terms, but the members can—and do—call for a national election at any time if there is a deadlock on a serious issue.

Every citizen, both Arab and Jew, over the age of 18 can vote in the national election of the Knesset. Nevertheless, usually only about eight Knesset members—less than 7 percent—are Arabs. Votes are cast for a party and its list of candidates rather than for individual district representatives. The number of candidates that each party sends to parliament depends on the percentage of the total national vote that party receives in the election.

Israel's president is elected by the parliament to a five-year term. Primarily fulfilling ceremonial duties, the president has little governmental power other than to appoint a prime minister, who serves as the head of government. The person who is chosen as prime minister traditionally is that party leader who is favored most by the Knesset. The prime minister heads the main executive body—a cabinet of about 15 ministers who are approved by the Knesset.

The nation's judiciary is composed of two systems—civil and religious. A 10-member supreme court and, beneath it, district, municipal, and magistrate's courts rule on civil matters. Most personal matters—such as marriages and divorces—are handled by religious courts. Jews, Muslims, and Christians each have their own courts.

Israel is divided into six local administrative districts. A commissioner, who is appointed by the central government, heads each district and is responsible to the minister of the interior. The Ministry of Defense administers the occupied territories.

Labor party leader Shimon Peres served as prime minister from 1984 to 1986 before turning the position over to Shamir.

Courtesy of Steve Feinstein

Beautiful flowers are an inexpensive purchase at an outdoor market in Tel Aviv-Jaffa. Israel exports most of its flowers to European markets.

3) The People

Comprising a minority of the population upon independence in 1948, Jews now make up about 85 percent of Israel's 4.4 million people. Israelis of Jewish heritage, however, come from diverse cultures throughout the world. Speaking different languages upon their arrival in Israel, many Jewish immigrants know little Hebrew—the primary national language. Under the Law of Return established upon independence, any Jew who immigrates to Israel is granted citizenship almost automatically. Only in rare instances is citizenship denied. Non-Jews may also im-migrate to Israel, but, as in most other countries, acquiring citizenship is a slow legal process.

Jews

Nearly 50 percent of Israel's Jews were born in the country. Another 25 percent were born in Europe and are referred to as Ashkenazim, or European Jews. The rest —generally called Sephardic Jews—came from other Middle Eastern or North African countries. Most of the first immigrants to Israel came from Europe, bringing with

38

These Jewish children have come to Israel from Ethiopia. More than 15,000 of Israel's newest immigrants have come from this East African country, in part to escape famine and war. The Ethiopian Jews refer to themselves as the "Beta Yisrael," or House of Israel.

them Western culture, technology, and attitudes that had a huge impact on the new nation's development.

After 1950, however, most of the Jewish immigrants came from the surrounding Arab-dominated world. The Sephardim differed greatly from their Western co-religionists. Physically, for example, they resembled the Arab population among whom they had lived. Furthermore, they spoke Arabic, and their attitudes and life-styles were Eastern, not Western. Consequently, two separate Jewish communities arose in Israel.

Like Israel's Arab minority, the Sephardim are generally less educated and have a lower economic status than the Ashkenazim. Adapting to Western culture has been difficult for these Eastern Jews. Some of them resent European Jews for not considering the contributions that the Sephardim—with their Eastern experience

Two Hasidic Jews—members of an extremely orthodox sect established in Poland during the mid-eighteenth century—converse near Jerusalem's Western Wall, Judaism's holiest site. Hasidic men wear long beards, hats called *shtreimel*, and long black coats, called *bekesheh*. Their joyous worship often includes singing and dancing.

In this orthodox Jewish home, the head of the family blesses the children on Yom Kippur—the Day of Atonement. Orthodox Jews follow a strict observance of Jewish custom. Men, for example, keep their heads covered at all times.

—could make, especially in relations with the rest of the Middle East.

Gradually, however, the Sephardim have been gaining greater influence in national affairs. The rise to power of the Likud party was partly a result of increased political awareness among Sephardim. Since the late 1970s, more Sephardim have held both local and national government positions, and their standard of living has begun to improve.

Another source of tension within the Jewish community is between orthodox (strict, traditional) Jews and other Jews—both moderately religious and secular (nonreligious). The orthodox Jews have pushed for a religious state that would operate according to the laws of the Torah, or the first five books of the Old Testament. Secular Jews—many of whom were born in Israel and consider themselves more Israeli than Jewish—believe in a political democracy and object to moves toward a religious state.

Arabs

The Arab population within the 1948 boundaries of Israel constitutes about 15 percent of the total population. In keeping with the separate traditions of Middle Eastern cultures, Jews and Arabs rarely live together in the same neighborhoods or even in the same towns. Nazareth, Haifa, and Jerusalem are exceptions to this rule. Jaffa, now a part of Tel Aviv–Jaffa, historically has been an Arab town, as has Acre, outside of Haifa. The area between the towns of Hadera and Afula has a large, rural-based Arab population. Arabs also

Israel's largest mosque, or Muslim house of worship, is al-Jazzar in the city of Acre. A muezzin, or crier, summons the faithful to prayer from a slender tower, or minaret *(foreground).*

Bedouin Arabs who continue their nomadic lifestyle dwell in tents fashioned from goat hair.

Some of the tensions between Arabs and Jews stem from the introduction into Israel of Western culture by Jews emigrating from Europe. These Arabs combine Western clothing with traditional Bedouin styles.

live in western Galilee north of Haifa and in parts of lower Galilee.

Mosques—Muslim houses of worship—are the distinctive landmarks of Arab villages. Many of these villages are built along hillsides to leave the best land for farming, olive groves, or vineyards. Arabs also have their own industries, centered in larger Arab towns such as Nazareth and Acre.

Nearly 10 percent of the Arabs in Israel are Bedouin, most of whom live in the Negev Desert. Traditionally the Bedouin have led a nomadic lifestyle, but they are slowly becoming settled in permanent communities as agriculture extends farther into the desert region.

Although Arabs living within Israel have benefited from mandatory education for boys and girls and from improved standards of living and health, many have been dissatisfied with life in the Jewish state. Getting used to Israel's Western culture has been difficult for them.

Israeli law has forced Arabs to end the Muslim practice of polygyny (the custom of a husband having more than one wife). They lack identification with national and religious holidays, and they have been excluded from the military and from certain government jobs. In addition, Arabs suffer discrimination in various areas of opportunity, such as buying land and receiving government funding. Although fear of Jewish retaliation once inhibited Arab political organization within Israel, Arabs increasingly support the Rakah, or New Communist party, in nonviolent protest against the established government.

The Occupied Areas

Following the Six-Day War in 1967, Israel assumed control over one million additional Arabs—650,000 in the West Bank formerly held by Jordan, 350,000 in the Gaza Strip, 33,000 in Sinai, and 6,000 in the Golan Heights. Israel maintains that the fate of these areas can be decided only by peace treaties between Israel and the Arab states.

LIVING CONDITIONS

The situation of the Arabs living under Israeli military occupation is complex. Arabs are under the rule of the Ministry of Defense, and, to discourage guerrilla activity, the Israeli government has at times made mass arrests, punished whole Arab communities for individual offenses, and mistreated suspects. Clashes between Israeli troops and Arabs are frequent. Arabs from the occupied areas are able to take jobs in Israel. Nevertheless, they do not receive wages as high as those received by the Israelis, unless they get their jobs through government labor exchanges.

Despite these hardships, the Arab standard of living has improved during the occupation. The Israeli government, in co-

At a suq, or outdoor market, an Arab woman looks over a wide selection of clothing.

An Arab village is nestled in a hillside in lower Galilee on the Israeli-occupied West Bank. Before the Six-Day War in 1967, this area was administered by Jordan. Arabs living in villages such as this one enjoy better health care and educational opportunities than they did before 1967, but many would prefer a return to Arab rule.

Courtesy of Steve Feinstein

Courtesy of Steve Feinstein

Despite the restrictions imposed on Palestinians who live in the occupied regions, Arabs are permitted to travel from the West Bank to Jordan via the Allenby Bridge.

operation with the UN Relief and Works Agency, has provided money and effort to improve the quality of health care, education, housing, and other welfare services available to the Arab population.

Furthermore, Arabs in the occupied territories have some political independence: they hold free local elections, and their laws are determined by their own courts. Despite this policy, however, when local Arab mayors sympathize with the PLO, Israelis remove them from office. Israel also maintains an "open bridges" policy along the Jordanian border, which allows Arabs from the West Bank to visit their Jordanian relatives and to trade with Jordan.

PALESTINIAN NATIONALISM

The renewed contact between Arabs from Israel proper and Arabs from the occupied areas has led to a heightened national awareness among Israeli Arabs, who identify more and more with their fellow Palestinians on the West Bank and in the Gaza Strip. During the 20 years of Israeli military occupation, frustrations have increased among both Arabs and Jews.

The result has been occasional, low-level guerrilla activity, which inflames Jewish-Arab relations and often begins cycles of violence and protest. In late 1987 Palestinian discontent erupted in an *intifadeh* (uprising) against the occupation. Armed with stones and firebombs, some Palestinians have lost their lives in clashes with Israeli soldiers since the intifadeh began.

The Palestinian Arabs want to gain national dignity by having their own country. But many Jews regard these areas as important to Israel's security needs, and some Jews further justify their claims to the territory on a historical and religious

A young, hearing-impaired Palestinian refugee learns to speak at a school for the deaf in Bethlehem, on the West Bank. He and his Palestinian classmates receive financial support from the UNRWA.

Courtesy of UNRWA

basis. Thus, some form of independent Palestinian Arab state seems virtually impossible to negotiate.

Israel has not annexed these territories, but if it does, the balance of power in Israel could change dramatically. Israel's Arab minority would rise from 15 to 40 percent, and over several decades the Arabs could easily become a majority because their population is growing more rapidly than the Jewish population. Thus, politics in the Jewish democracy could become dominated by Arabs, endangering the very foundation of the State of Israel. Although most Israelis want peace, they are unwilling to give up territory until a solution is found that provides adequate security for the country.

The Army

Any Jew who comes to Israel to live can, under the Law of Return, acquire citizenship almost automatically. But citizenship means more than having the proper official papers. Israel's army has done the primary job of transforming new immigrants into citizens.

All Israeli men—with the exception of many of those studying in religious seminaries—and all unmarried women undergo military training. They are drafted at age 18, the men for three years, the women for two years. In addition, every man in the country who is fit must serve about four weeks a year in the active reserves until age 55. Unmarried women and women with no children serve in the reserves until age

Courtesy of CARE

This young Arab trains at a vocational school for a future career as a craftsperson.

34. Some women hold positions of military responsibility, such as teaching young recruits how to operate tanks, armed vehicles, and cannons.

Far more is taught in the army than military matters. For example, all new immigrants learn Hebrew, which ensures that Israeli citizens share a common language. In addition, the army teaches courses on the geography and history of Israel, as well as on basic arithmetic, health, and hygiene. Compulsory courses are given in citizenship and democracy.

Education

Free adult education courses in Hebrew, hygiene, vocational training, and other subjects are taught throughout Israel—at police stations, child-care clinics, and concert halls. Traveling schoolteachers make regular visits to absorption centers, where immigrants learn about life in Israel. Although only 48 percent of the Arab population is able to read and write, 88 percent of the Jewish population is literate.

Independent Picture Service

The Israeli army provides the equivalent of a primary education to every soldier who lacks one. For those who seek a high school diploma, the army offers special evening courses.

Primary education is free and compulsory for all children from the ages of 5 to 15. The state-funded schools include three educational systems: secular (nonreligious) schools, religious schools, and Arab-speaking schools. Although high school in Israel is not compulsory, it is free, and about 80 percent of the pupils graduating from primary school continue their education. Israel's institutions of higher learning are the Technion, Weizmann Institute, Hebrew University of Jerusalem, Tel Aviv University, Haifa University, Bar-Ilan University, and Ben-Gurion University in Beersheba.

The Histadrut

The main institution in Israel during its early years was the Histadrut, or General Federation of Labor. Created by the Zionist workers' movement in the first two decades of the twentieth century, the Histadrut has three major areas of activity.

First, the Histadrut is a federation of trade unions whose membership includes

Independent Picture Service

Military training for women is compulsory in the Israeli army. This woman is a parachutist.

45

The main campus of Jerusalem's Hebrew University—located at the top of Mount Scopus—offers degrees in education and business as well as in general studies.

about 90 percent of all wage earners. Including families, it covers two-thirds of the entire Jewish population and about one-quarter of the Arab population within Israel's pre-1967 borders. Confronted with the task of absorbing masses of immigrants into the Israeli work force, the Histadrut gives all new members—including Arabs—the same rights and privileges enjoyed by veteran workers. The Histadrut strives to balance the nation's economic needs and rate of growth with the welfare of Israeli workers.

Second, the Histadrut is the nation's largest employer. Most agricultural and industrial cooperatives are affiliated with *Hevrat Ha-Ovdim* (Worker's Society—the production division of the Histadrut). In addition, Hevrat Ha-Ovdim owns some of Israel's largest enterprises and works in partnership with private business and the government.

The third activity of the Histadrut is to organize social services and to introduce progressive social legislation. A health insurance plan operated by *Kupat Holim* (the Histadrut health fund) covers about 75 percent of the total population, and 80 percent of all the wage earners are on Histadrut pension plans. The Histadrut also operates a social security center to combat poverty and to aid the underprivileged. The *Mishan* (support) social welfare center helps needy members and their families by providing services for orphans, single-parent families, the elderly, and the unemployed. Finally, the Histadrut provides free adult and youth education.

Health Care

Israel has a ratio of one doctor for every 415 people, which represents one of the best doctor-patient ratios in the world.

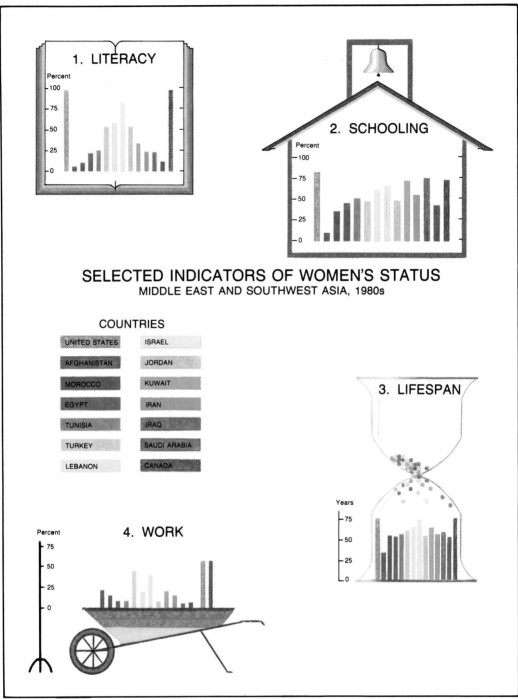

SELECTED INDICATORS OF WOMEN'S STATUS
MIDDLE EAST AND SOUTHWEST ASIA, 1980s

Artwork by Carol F. Barrett

Depicted in this chart are factors relating to the status of women in the Middle East and southwest Asia. Graph 1, labeled Literacy, shows the percentage of adult women who can read and write. Graph 2 illustrates the proportion of school-aged girls who actually attend elementary and secondary schools. Graph 3 depicts the life expectancy of female babies at birth. Graph 4 shows the percentage of women in the income-producing work force. Data taken from *Women in the World: An International Atlas*, 1986 and from *Women . . . A World Survey*, 1985.

A mobile clinic provides medical services to the citizens of an Arab town.

More than 9,000 physicians and 20,000 nurses practice medicine in Israel. The excellent doctor-patient ratio and the benefits of modernization have increased life expectancy in Israel to 75 years of age, a figure similar to those in developed countries of the Western world. The infant mortality rate of 11.2 for every 1,000 live births also compares well with Western figures and is in sharp contrast to the average of 89 per 1,000 for western Asia.

The Israeli government owns 25 percent of Israel's 145 hospitals and 65 percent of the 870 child-care centers. Most workers have access, through the Histadrut, to the Kupat Holim medical service. This service provides complete medical care and runs several hospitals. Ninety-five percent of the Israeli population is covered by some form of health care.

Religion

Although about 85 percent of all Israelis are Jewish, other major religions are also practiced within the country. Of the Arab population, 78 percent are Muslim, 14 percent are Christian, and 8 percent are Druze—a secretive Islamic sect that has developed its own traditions, taking some elements from both Judaism and Christianity. Several different sects—such as Greek Catholic, Greek Orthodox, Maronite, and Protestant—make up the Christian population.

Israeli law guarantees freedom of religion for every citizen. Each religious community is allowed to observe its weekly Sabbath and its holidays. Religious councils and courts govern the personal affairs of each community. The Ministry of Religious Affairs is charged with meeting each community's needs, including financial assistance for religious institutions, education, councils, and courts. The ministry also supervises all holy sites in cooperation with the religious authorities responsible for each site.

Because Israel is a state for Jews, most cities and towns observe some Jewish practices. On the Jewish Sabbath, from Friday night to Saturday night, public transportation stops in many towns, and cafes and other public places close. Jewish dietary laws are followed in all public institutions—such as the army, government buildings, hospitals, and schools—and in most restaurants and hotels. The Jewish holidays of Rosh Hashanah (New Year), Yom Kippur (Day of Atonement), Hanukkah (Festival of Lights), and Pesach (Passover) are celebrated as national holidays.

Although conflicts between Jews and Christians rarely arise in Israel, occasional problems break out between Jews and Muslims over access rights to shared religious sites. During the past 50 years, major disputes have erupted over the Temple Mount area and the Western Wall in Jerusalem and over the Cave of the Machpelah in Hebron on the West Bank. The cave is believed to be the burial site of the biblical prophets Abraham, Isaac, Jacob,

Mosques hold prayer services five times a day. Here, a group of men pray in the direction of Mecca, the city in Saudi Arabia where Muhammad, the founder of Islam, was born.

Independent Picture Service

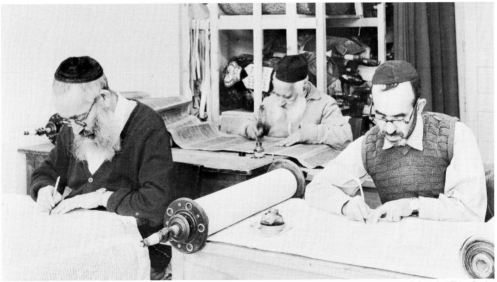

Independent Picture Service

The Torah—a collection of Jewish scripture used in all synagogues—must be hand-copied with a feather pen on special parchment. The finished scroll is checked to be sure that every Hebrew letter is identical to the original. Sections of the Torah are chanted aloud in the synagogue on Monday and Thursday mornings, on the Sabbath, and on special holidays.

49

Courtesy of Israel Government Tourism Administration

Marc Chagall—one of the twentieth century's most renowned painters and graphic artists—created these stained-glass windows depicting the 12 tribes of Israel for the synagogue at Hebrew University Medical Center in Jerusalem. A Russian-born Jew, Chagall often used biblical stories as the subject matter for his work.

and their respective wives Sarah, Rebecca, and Leah, who are revered by Muslims and Jews alike.

Literature and Art

The most prominent of the first Hebrew writers were the poets Haim Nahman Bialik and Saul Tchernichovsky and the novelist S. Y. Agnon, who won the 1966 Nobel Prize for literature. During the 1950s, prose, poetry, and novels focused on Zionist themes and on the Holocaust. Since then writers have dealt with more modern topics in their fiction. The most significant recent writers are Amos Oz and A. B. Yehoshua.

Although nonreligious practices tend to dominate the life of many Israelis, most can identify with the strong Judaic expressions that still pervade literature. Many motifs come directly from the Bible but take on new symbolic meaning.

Israeli achievement in fine arts is centered around the Bezalel School of the Arts and Crafts. Founded in Jerusalem by

Courtesy of Israel Government Tourism Administration

The menorah is a ritual symbol from biblical times. During the rededication of the temple in Jerusalem in 165 B.C., only one small vessel of oil could be found, but the small quantity burned for eight days. In modern times, the menorah is lit for eight days in December at Hanukkah to commemorate the ancient event.

Boris Shatz—who emigrated from Bulgaria at the turn of the twentieth century—the school has attempted to blend modern Western and traditional Jewish artistic images. During the 1930s, immigrant artists from Germany provided a Germanic influence that greatly affected Israeli architecture. Since the 1950s, Israeli art has generally shifted between an emphasis on Jewish traditions and on participation in an international art style. Reuvin Rubin, Joseph Zaritzky, Mordechai Ardon, and Yaacov Agam are among the best-known Israeli painters of the past 30 years.

Independent Picture Service
This painter is a member of an artists' village established at Ein Haud, near the port city of Haifa.

Courtesy of Israel Government Tourism Administration
Builders of the highway along the shores of the Dead Sea have created modern sculptures using boulders cleared from the road's path.

The Performing Arts

During the early years of the state, music in Israel was based largely on folk music, much of which was derived from the Bible. The pioneering spirit of the country fostered cultural expressions that were nonreligious and free-spirited. Some folk dances were influenced by Arab music and dance, and others were blended from the mixed traditions of Eastern Europe and the Middle East.

By the 1960s a new tradition emerged—popular music that maintained ties to the

Jerusalem's Shrine of the Book houses the Dead Sea Scrolls. The curved, white-tiled roof symbolizes the lid of the jar in which the scrolls were discovered in 1947. The contrast between the white building and the stark, black marble slab represents the views of the Essenes, an ancient people of Khirbat Qumran (where the scrolls were found) who believed they were struggling between the forces of light and the forces of darkness.

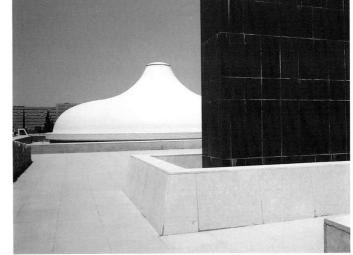
Courtesy of Steve Feinstein

Western influence on Israel's musical forms finds expression in the nation's Philharmonic Orchestra, seen here performing at the Mann Auditorium in Tel Aviv–Jaffa.

folk tradition. Shoshana Damari and Dov Seltzer helped start the folk movement. In recent years, Chava Alberstein, Ofra Haza, Shlomo Artzi, and Yardena Arazi have become popular.

In the realm of classical music, a strong tradition began during the 1930s when Palestine became a place of refuge for hundreds of Jewish musicians who fled Nazi-dominated Europe. The Palestine

Members of a Hasidic dance troupe (above) perform a dance of Eastern European origin. The Batsheva Dance Company (left) is one of Israel's foremost modern dance troupes.

Symphony Orchestra, now called the Israel Philharmonic, was founded in 1936. The immigration of Soviet Jews to Israel during the 1970s and early 1980s provided a substantial pool of individuals with strong musical training, and several new orchestras were established.

Israel boasts five major theater companies that present plays with a classical background as well as plays with Jewish themes. The Habimah, based in Tel Aviv since 1932, is the national theater. The Cameri Theater, established in 1944 and also based in Tel Aviv, was the first theater to deal with local, Israeli topics. The Haifa and Beersheba municipal theaters do repertory performances. Israel also has a Children's and Youth Theater and a Kibbutz Theater.

Sports

Soccer and basketball rank as the nation's most popular team sports. Professional as well as amateur leagues exist for both of these activities. Israel also competes in soccer internationally and has won the European Cup Basketball Championship twice. In recent years, major tennis competitions have been held in Israel. Shlomo Glickstein and Amos Mansdorf, Israeli professional tennis players, were both

During the annual Passover season, over 20,000 Israeli soldiers and civilians join in the March to Jerusalem. The impressive gathering symbolizes national unity as well as progress.

Shoppers stroll by a colorful market in Jerusalem *(right)*. **An Arab suq** *(above)* **features endless varieties of baskets and handbags made of straw.**

ranked among the top 35 players in the world during the mid-1980s.

Perhaps Israel's true sports hobby is hiking. Israelis love to learn about their country on foot, and they take to the roads and hiking trails in large numbers. A popular event in Israel is an annual trek to Jerusalem that lasts from two to four days, with thousands of participants ranging in age from 15 to 70.

Another favorite event is the Jewish Olympics, or Maccabiah Games. Held every four years in the impressive 60,000-seat Ramat Gan Stadium outside Tel Aviv, the games attract Jewish sports clubs from all over the world.

Three Palestinian men stand beside their colorfully decorated truck.

Traditionally the mainstay of Israel's agriculture, the kibbutz has recently turned to industry as well. Members earn no salaries; rather, in exchange for their labor, all needs are met by the budget of the kibbutz.

4) The Economy

During its early years of statehood Israel's economy was almost nonexistent, since the neighboring Arab countries—its chief source of food and oil—refused to trade directly with the new nation. Nevertheless, the country was faced with feeding and housing a huge wave of new immigrants, who doubled the state's population within four years. Agriculture produced barely enough for the severely rationed population.

Israel's industrial exports during its first years consisted of small shipments of citrus by-products, polished diamonds, textiles, pharmaceuticals, and false teeth. In the realm of mineral resources, only potash production along the Dead Sea had been developed. Chances for Israel's future industrial growth looked extremely dim.

But direct and immediate aid to the new state came from Jews in other countries. The assistance included Israeli State Bonds, German payments for crimes against victims of the Holocaust (paid to Israel as trustee for those Jews who were killed during the period from 1939 to 1945), and grants from the United States and other governments.

Economic Conditions in the 1980s

The biggest problem to plague Israel during the 1980s was inflation, caused by the country's enormous spending on defense and by the people's strong appetite for consumer goods. During the late 1970s and early 1980s, the government of Prime Minister Menachem Begin actually encouraged the population to spend in the hope of creating sufficient support among the Israeli voters to reelect the Likud bloc.

Israel's balance of payments became so bad during 1983 and 1984 that inflation skyrocketed. By January 1985 the annual rate of inflation had reached 400 percent. The impact on the average Israeli, however, was not as great as might be imagined, because the government raised workers' wages to match the rate of inflation. Such a reckless policy, however, almost bankrupted the country.

During 1985 the government of Shimon Peres finally began to curb inflation by reducing the linkage between wages and price rises and by establishing strict price controls on essential products. Peres also raised tariffs on imported goods and charged Israelis a tax to limit travel until the national crisis was over. By the beginning of 1987 the intensive campaign to control the economy began to work, and the inflation rate came down to a manageable 20 percent for the year.

Agriculture

Israel's dry climate posed a tremendous challenge to early Jewish settlers. With the aid of scientific research and advanced technology, however, Israel has developed irrigation and land reclamation programs, which make more land suitable for farm-

Courtesy of Steve Feinstein

Courtesy of Steve Feinstein

Rapid evaporation of water in the Negev Desert *(above)* **produces deep cracks in the dried ground. Water-transport plans and drip-irrigation systems have significantly increased agricultural yields** *(left).*

Most of the central Negev is rocky desert. The topsoil, however, is composed of loess—a crumbly mixture of silt, sand, and clay that can be reclaimed with sufficient water. On the Ein Gedi kibbutz—a successful reclamation project—tomatoes flourish under plastic covers.

ing. In 1952, for example, the Hula swamp north of the Sea of Galilee was drained and opened up for agricultural use.

In addition, the National Water Carrier project moves water from the Sea of Galilee to the southern part of the country. The plan includes a number of regional projects, such as the pipeline completed in 1964 that runs from the Sea of Galilee to the Negev Desert. Drip-irrigation systems, which strategically supply water just to the roots of plants, have also been developed. As a result of these schemes, Israel has increased its agricultural production more than sixfold, and the nation now produces 75 percent of its food requirements.

Farming varies from area to area within Israel. On the coastal plain and adjoining valleys, vegetables, poultry, fruit, and grapes are the main yields. In the sub-tropical area around Bet She'an and the Jordan River Valley, banana plantations and commercial fish breeding are found. In Galilee, olive and tobacco plantations prevail. Apple orchards do well in upper Galilee because of the cool evenings in the region during the fall and winter. Cotton also has become a major crop in the north. In addition, Israel has developed excellent dairy cattle, and milk production per cow is among the highest in the world.

Some farms in Israel are privately owned, but most farmers belong to either cooperative or collective communities. In cooperative communities, called moshavim, each family works its own patch of land and lives in private homes. The village administration markets everyone's produce and provides each family with equipment and supplies.

Teenagers living and working on a kibbutz learn early the responsibilities of adulthood. Although most young people in kibbutzim now live with their parents, children have separate areas where they can spend time with friends after school until their parents come home from work.

Collective communities, called kibbutzim, also pool their produce, which they own and market as a group. They differ from moshavim in that the kibbutz provides completely for everyone's needs and everything is shared. Kibbutzim farmers share property and combine their labor.

Adults and children traditionally have separate eating and sleeping quarters. Children are raised together and learn at an early age that community needs are more important than family needs. Many kibbutz families, however, have begun to live in their own private living quarters.

Fishponds on a kibbutz add to the many foodstuffs produced on these agricultural settlements.

Courtesy of Steve Feinstein

Photo by Nancy Durrell McKenna

Volunteers from around the world come to work on kibbutzim every year.

Diamond cutting is a major source of revenue for Israel. Here, experts classify industrial diamonds at the Diamond Exchange in Ramat Gan.

An agricultural center grows an alga known as spiralina in a giant tank. Spiralina has proven to be a nutritious food supplement and is also used in the manufacture of some chemicals and dyes.

Manufacturing

About 25 percent of Israel's labor force is employed in manufacturing, and industry accounts for 20 percent of the gross national product (GNP). Although Israel began with only a few manufacturing companies, by the 1970s the nation had hundreds of flourishing industrial enterprises, which represented the fastest-growing sector of the economy.

Some of the most important industries produce chemicals, pharmaceuticals, cut and polished diamonds, textiles, and processed foods. Israel imports rough diamonds from South Africa and cuts and polishes them into small gems used in jewelry. Diamonds are Israel's largest export, and the nation is second only to Belgium in its output of the processed gems.

Since 1975 the kibbutz, traditionally an agricultural unit, has undergone a process of rural industrialization. Each kibbutz that was interested in manufacturing developed a planning board to seek out the best industry to locate on its ground. The result is a widespread pattern of rural industry, which includes factories for items like machine tools, cables, wire, electrical circuit boards, irrigation systems, furniture, and processed food for overseas sales. Products of the 330 kibbutzim account for 5 percent of Israel's industrial output. The presence of factories has provided kibbutzim with income to carry them through slow agricultural seasons.

The Armaments Industry

Another area of the economy that has grown is the production and sale of military equipment. The constant threat of war that Israel lives with and the unreliability of foreign sources of arms forced the nation to develop its own weapons industry. Although arms are still Israel's largest import, the nation has reduced its need to import military equipment and can design products to meet its own needs. Israelis produce and export small weapons —including the Uzi submachine gun and navy-based missile systems—as well as improve designs of tanks and aircraft made in other countries. The defense industry employs thousands of Israelis.

Mineral and Energy Resources

Many valuable mineral resources—such as potash, copper, granite, and phosphate—have been found in the Dead Sea and in the Negev Desert. Of the chemical salts taken from the Dead Sea, potash—used mainly in fertilizers—is the most important. Bromine, which is used in making drugs and other products, is another major resource extracted from the Dead Sea.

Small quantities of oil were discovered in Israel during the 1950s, but the nation produces less than 10 percent of the petroleum it uses and imports the rest. During its occupation of the Sinai Peninsula from 1967 to 1982, Israel controlled and developed the Abu Rudeis oil fields, but gave back this valuable resource to Egypt as part of the peace agreement between

Egypt and Israel. Many regions of Israel have undertaken experimental drilling projects. Because Israel's soil is similar to that of other parts of the Middle East, geologists think that larger quantities of oil will probably be discovered.

Israel's sunny weather is ideal for the use of solar energy, and the country is one of the largest per capita consumers of solar energy in the world. About 25 percent of all households have installed solar water-heating systems, and some are beginning to use thermal energy to power electricity and air-conditioning as well.

International Trade

Since its birth in 1948, Israel has been heavily dependent on outside sources for consumer products and financial assistance. This situation has created an imbalanced economy in which Israel spends much more money than it earns. In the mid-1980s the nation's imports exceeded $8.5 billion, and exports were only $5.1 billion. As a result, the national debt is over $15 billion.

Israel imports most of its raw materials, including precious metals, chemical products, oil, coal, machinery, industrial equipment, and rough diamonds. In addition, it spends millions of dollars each year

A worker logs information at the potash research station on the Dead Sea. The body of water is one of the world's greatest sources of the important mineral.

Independent Picture Service

Good transport arrangements between Israel and Europe have contributed to the strong growth of citrus exports to the continent. Exports doubled in the period between 1970 and 1983.

on foreign-made armaments. Principal suppliers of these items are the United States, West Germany, Belgium, Luxembourg, Great Britain, and Switzerland.

Exports include electrical and nonelectrical machinery, polished diamonds, agrotechnology, irrigation systems, computer software, medical electronics, solar energy systems, chemicals, textiles, clothing, and leather. Citrus fruits, flowers, fruit juices, wines and liquors, and sweets are also important exports. Israeli markets cover most of the globe, including North and South America, Europe, and many nations in Africa and Asia. In addition to consumer products, Israelis provide extensive technical expertise to developing countries.

Tourism

Over one million tourists visit Israel each year, providing the country with a major source of foreign currency. Israel offers a unique setting that appeals to the religious

The Dead Sea is of economic benefit both to industry – because of its vast mineral deposits – and to tourism. During the winter, visitors vacation at health resorts along the Dead Sea's shores.

Decades of political and religious conflict have pitted Arab against Jew. This view of Jerusalem's Old City symbolizes the hope many share of a resolution that will allow both groups to coexist peacefully in this city sacred to Muslims, Christians, and Jews.

pilgrim, to the sunbather, to the person schooled in history, or to someone interested in a modern, technological society. Archaeological sites attract people from many countries. The Old City of Jerusalem contains numerous places of religious interest to Muslims, Jews, and Christians who travel to Israel.

Resorts along the Mediterranean coast provide fun and relaxation for thousands of tourists. The Tel Aviv–Jaffa coast is often referred to as "East Miami Beach" because of its resemblance to the famous city in the United States. New, modern, air-conditioned hotels have been built all over the country. Israeli hotels were often at full capacity until the upsurge of inter-

national terrorism during 1984 and 1985 decreased tourism.

The Future

Despite the problems of war and peace, Israel has managed to create a modern economy with a standard of living comparable to that of Western European countries and well ahead of the Middle Eastern region. Although Israel is not at peace on all fronts, it has established itself as a major military power in the Middle East. It remains to be seen what, if any, solution can be worked out to settle the disputed territories and to create a homeland for the displaced Palestinian Arabs.

Index